SO, YOU THINK YOUR KID IS PSYCHIC?

BY: MATTHEW & LEITREANNA BROWN, JUDY TERRY, BLAINE ROHAN, & GWEN JOHNS

You are a child of the Universe, no less than the moon and the stars; you have a right to be here. And whether or not it is clear to you, no doubt the Universe is unfolding as it should. ("Desiderata: Original Text")
— Max Ehrmann, American Poet

Your Psychic Connection.

By Leitreanna Brown,

Cover design by Leitreanna Brown

Edited and formatted by VAPBooks,

VAPBooks Publishing, Virginia, USA.

Table of Contents

Dedication 5

Acknowledgement................................7

Introduction 8

Where Do Psychic Abilities Come From? Is This Psychic Stuff Real? 10

The Case of the Shadows: A Psychic Child's Unseen Guests 14

Do I Need to be Psychic to be a Good Parent to My Psychic Kid?..18

Beyond the Veil: Government Ventures into Psychic Phenomena 23

NASA's Remote Sensing: Science and Perception.......24

How Do I Find Out If My Family and I Have Psychic Abilities? 28

Was My Family Different?.................................35

The Science of Inheritance: Epigenetics and Spiritual Sensitivity..38

A Sacred Responsibility 40

Does My Child Have Spiritual Gifts? How Would I Know? Are There Signs? 42

The Ghost Gwen Never Asked For 51

The Woman in the Cemetery.................................53

The Weight of Being Different 55

Finding the Circle..56

Reflection Journal: Reclaiming What Was Hidden 58

"How do I protect my child from people that will not understand or from negative entities?" 60

The Soul, The Gift, and The Legacy 70

"How Do I Nurture My Child's Psychic Gifts?" 71

"Where Do I Go From Here?" 75

My Family Was Different 77

Testing Spirits....................................79

More About the Science of Inheritance......................81

How This Relates to Psychic Sensitivity......................83

Inheriting More Than DNA.............................86

Key Scientific Findings Supporting Epigenetic Inheritance 87

Epigenetics and Psychic Families 90

Nature, Nurture, and the Soul.......................92

A Sacred Responsibility 94

The Parent as Guardian of the Gift: Your Sacred Role in Raising a Psychic Child...........................95

Further Guidance: 100

You are Not Alone in This 101

Closing Thoughts 102

ABOUT THE AUTHORS............................110

Dedication

We—Matthew, Blaine, Judy, Gwen and I—dedicate this book to our families, whose love and support have been the foundation of this journey.
Blaine wishes to give special acknowledgment to his beloved Jennifer, Brittany, and Penny. Your unwavering presence in his life has been a source of strength and inspiration.

For me, this book is also dedicated to my dear friend, Gwen. You have been a steadfast pillar of love, patience, and encouragement. Your support has carried us through the unknown, and your kindness has helped light the way.

To Matthew—your courage, wisdom, and compassion continue to illuminate the path for so many. Thank you for your unwavering belief in the unseen. Your strength in embracing the mysteries of life has inspired us all to face the unknown with open hearts. Your deep respect for both spiritual and physical realms reminds us that true healing begins when we honor both with humility and grace.

We offer our deepest gratitude to Shaman Willie Gibson. Your timeless wisdom, your connection to the ancestors, and your reverence for all living things have been a guiding light. Your teachings have shown us the sacred balance between worlds and the healing power that comes from love, humility, and service. It is because of you we understand the importance of nurturing gifts within our families and within ourselves.

We are honored to carry forward the traditions you so generously share and offer this work as a tribute to your spirit and the sacred journey you continue to walk.

Acknowledgement

We honor the spirits who have walked beside us—Janawa, Minne, and the Colonel—whose gentle guidance and protective presence have nurtured our hearts and shielded us on countless paranormal investigations. Their unseen hands have helped us connect with the world beyond and approach every encounter with reverence and courage.

We also give thanks to the many students who have trusted us to guide their journeys, the families who opened their homes and hearts, and the spirits who have revealed themselves in moments of profound stillness. Each experience has deepened our understanding and connected us to the vast, mysterious tapestry of existence. It is through this shared exploration that we grow together, through the threshold of the known and unknown.

Introduction

Raising children has always been a subject drenched in passion, hope, and the timeless quest for understanding. In every corner of the world, parents sift through cultural wisdom, religious teachings, realities, and family legacies, all trying to craft a life that nurtures their children's full potential. We hear voices of psychiatrists and sociologists debating the age-old nature versus nurture question, weighing genetic destiny against environmental shaping.

Amidst this vast conversation, something extraordinary quietly unfolds in some homes: children awakening to the mystical, the psychic, and the spiritual gifts that seem to pulse beneath the surface of ordinary life. These gifts do not discriminate—they emerge regardless of social status, race, nationality, or upbringing. The presence of these abilities challenges our understanding of reality and forces families to navigate uncharted waters.

Many parents find themselves caught in the bewildering crossroads where love meets fear. How do you protect a child from things you cannot see or understand? When a child predicts events yet to come, speaks to invisible friends, or experiences night terrors tied to the house's dark history, the ground beneath your feet shifts.

This book is a gentle invitation to sit with us, to find comfort in shared stories, to learn practical ways to nurture and protect your gifted child. Pour your coffee, settle in — let us explore together what it means to live with psychic children.

Where Do Psychic Abilities Come From? Is This Psychic Stuff Real?

Blaine's reflection on the question.

So, you have started to sense that your child may have psychic gifts. It is a feeling that reaches beyond logic—an intuition that something sacred is stirring within them. These gifts are not coincidences. They are like seeds planted in the soul before birth, waiting for the right moment to bloom. Often, they emerge in early childhood, but just as often, they awaken after a life-altering event—a move, a deployment, a deep loss, or a family separation. When a child's world shifts, their spirit searches for new anchors. In that tender space of vulnerability, the veil between worlds can grow thin.

In those moments, something beautiful happens: a child's awareness expands. Like the sky at dawn, their consciousness stretches wide, and their natural-born abilities begin to shine through—subtle at first, then undeniable. It can be awe-inspiring, even startling. And yet, these gifts are delicate. They can fade. They can be silent. Often, they are lost not through denial, but through fear of judgment, fear of misunderstanding, fear of being different.

One of the deepest heartbreaks we see is when a child, surrounded by fear they did not create, begins to believe that *they* are the reason others are uncomfortable. Just like children of divorce may blame themselves for a family's pain, psychic children often internalize the fear around them. And in doing so, they shut down their gifts. They dim their own light to make others feel safer.

But this dimming is a quiet tragedy—not just for the child, but for the world.

Psychic gifts are meant to be honored, protected, and nurtured. They are part of the divine blueprint of who we are. And yet, what happens when a child senses something others don't—an approaching death, a glimpse of suffering, or an unspoken truth? Imagine the weight of that knowledge. Imagine the loneliness of carrying something too heavy for words, especially in a world that you may not believe or want to understand.

Some children are blamed. Some are shunned. Some are called cursed. These are the hard, painful realities psychic families have faced for generations.

But this does not have to be your child's path.

As parents, we hold a sacred duty—not to control the gift, but to guide our children gently through it. Help them understand what is theirs to carry and what is not. Teach them the power of prayer, of meditation, of connecting to something greater than themselves. Show them that knowledge—no matter how heavy—can be met with love. That even in the face of darkness, they are never powerless. That their prayers, their light, and their compassion can reach beyond the visible world.

Psychic gifts are not accidents. They are divine inheritances—given with purpose by a higher power, rooted in love and grace. Nearly every major religion acknowledges these gifts: prophecy, discernment, healing, visions. They are as natural as music, math, or art—only tuned to the spirit.

Matthew, Lei, Judy, and I stand with you because we have walked this path ourselves. I remember the loneliness of silence, the weight of knowing, and the ache of feeling different. But I also remember the moment I realized I was not alone.

You are not alone either.

We walk with you—with empathy, understanding, and hope. Your journey matters. Your child's gift is real. And together, we can protect it, nurture it, and watch it shine.

The Case of the Shadows: A Psychic Child's Unseen Guests

About eight years ago, a mother reached out to me with a desperate plea. Her young son's psychic gifts were spiraling beyond control. A self-proclaimed psychic "expert" had promised help but vanished, leaving the family adrift.

The boy's night terrors worsened; shadows in the home grew thicker, darker. Spirits haunted not just the house but the nearby schoolyard and the wooded path beyond the street. His world was no longer safe. The family, overwhelmed and frightened, moved their beds into the family room, seeking comfort in numbers.

They sought help from psychics and paranormal groups without relief until I stepped in and called Matthew and Leitreanna to assist.

Our first investigation revealed the first "shadow" was not a spirit at all, but a curious trick of light. A neighbor's stained-glass rocking horse hanging in an open sliding glass door reflected against the glass, casting a spectral figure on the boy's pathway at sunset. This reflection only appeared in spring and fall, disappearing when seasons changed and the neighbor closed the door.

But the school spirits proved more elusive. The boy described two child spirits—one was a barefoot girl in a simple dress resembling his grandmother's old nightgown, the other, a boy wearing overalls, both smeared with red dirt. The area around the school was lush green pasture, far from any red mud.

We combed old newspapers and property records, discovering a distant farm two miles away with a creek surrounded by red clay soil.

Lei took the boy to the deserted school grounds to call to the spirits, gently coaxing them forward. Matthew and Blaine examined the records and aerial views, while Lei helped the child learn to remote view.

Together, we journeyed through the ether to find the spirits, discovering a tragic history of two children who had vanished over a century ago.

The spirits' mother had drowned them in a muddy puddle outside their bedroom window after punishing them for defying authority and shirking chores. The children played in the mud puddle instead of digging potatoes. The mom felt the kids did not earn their food, so they would not get any. She said the children were a burden on the farm, so she eliminated them. The father, a grief-stricken spirit himself, appeared in the home, watching over his lost children and grateful for the family's kindness.

The boy's night terrors mirrored the trauma of the spirits' deaths. The night terrors included muddy water, thunder, and the feeling of being held down. As we healed the spiritual wounds, the family grew stronger. The shadows faded, replaced by light and peace.

We share these stories to remind you: psychic gifts connect us to worlds unseen, but they are not curses. With love, protection, and understanding, these gifts can become sources of strength and healing.

"When a child gives you a gift, even if it is just a rock that they just picked up. Show gratitude."
~Dean Jackson

Do I Need to be Psychic to be a Good Parent to My Psychic Kid?

Matt's Reflection

I have asked myself this question countless times over the years, especially in those quiet moments after the kids were tucked into bed and the house settled into a hush. Raising my children, brothers, sisters, nieces, and nephews, who possess such powerful, undeniable spiritual gifts, has been both a privilege and a profound challenge. I often wonder: Am I doing enough? Am I utterly understanding the depth of their experiences? Am I holding space for their unique journey in a way that honors who they are and what they carry within them?

My children's gifts are not just fleeting flashes of intuition or childish fantasies. They have vivid, detailed memories that do not seem to belong to this lifetime. Together, they recount stories, shared history of places, people, and time long past. When we take family trips to museums or wander through antique stores, they effortlessly identify artifacts, tools, and relics, describing not just what the objects are but how they were used, who might have held them, and the emotions that still cling to those items like a faint whisper. It is as if they are walking with echoes of the past, living bridges to forgotten lives.

These experiences blew my mind. There were nights when, my wife Leitreanna, Judy Terry, my mother-in-law, and Virginia Scott, my grandmother-in-law, and I sat quietly around the kitchen table, holding hands as our children led us through the vast spiritual menagerie they navigated with ease. We became more than a family; we became a circle, a psychic kids' support group of sorts. Each night, we shared the inexplicable events, the feelings, the symbols that appeared—trying to make sense of this unseen world our children were so deeply entwined with.

Something remarkable unfolded. We noticed patterns—clues that pointed backward into history, intertwining with our family lineage and stories. The spiritual phenomena were not random. They were threaded through time, connecting us to ancestors and events that shaped us long before our births. Each clue was a whisper from the past, beckoning us to investigate, to uncover hidden truths. Our lives changed. One by one, the adults in our family experienced psychic moments themselves. It was as if the gifts passed quietly through generations, awakening anew as we dared to open our hearts.

We soon realized that we were no longer just parents or grandparents. We were fellow travelers on a journey that blurred the boundaries between the physical and spiritual worlds. We learned you do not need to be "psychic" in the traditional sense to be a good parent to a psychic child. What matters deeply is your willingness to listen—really listen— and to hold your child's experiences without judgment or fear.

At the core, all humans have some measure of supernatural instinct. It is as natural as animals sensing danger or birds migrating with invisible maps etched in their minds. You do not have to be a seer or a mystic to support your child. You simply need to offer emotional validation. This means learning to understand their feelings, no matter how strange or frightening they might seem. Accepting those feelings lets your child know they are seen, heard, and loved exactly as they are.

Emotional validation is a quiet superpower. It tells your child, "I believe you. You matter. Your world is real." And that, more than any psychic talent, builds the foundation for a healthy, grounded life. When you hold that space, you give your child the freedom to explore and develop their gifts safely.

Sometimes parents worry they are not "gifted enough" to guide their psychic children, but you have another incredible strength: the gift of analysis, research, and unconditional love. Learning together, seeking knowledge about psychic phenomena, and sharing that journey with your child builds trust and connection.

So, why do many of us still whisper about psychic talents in hushed tones? Why do these extraordinary gifts remain hidden or misunderstood in public life?

The truth is, we are at the cusp of a new era, where millions are waking to the supernatural realities woven into our world.

If you are reading this, know that you are not alone. You are part of a growing family of awakened souls who have been blessed—and sometimes burdened—with knowledge beyond the ordinary. We are fortunate to have individual experiences that others can only dream of.

The Universe has a beautiful way of delivering exactly what you need at precisely the right time.

Beyond the Veil: Government Ventures into Psychic Phenomena

It might astonish you to learn that the U.S. government has actively explored psychic phenomena for decades. During the Cold War, the CIA and the Defense Intelligence Agency (DIA) initiated the Stargate Project—a clandestine program aimed at investigating the potential of psychic abilities, notably "remote viewing," for intelligence purposes. Remote viewing is the purported ability to perceive distant or unseen targets without the use of the traditional five senses. This program, involving collaborations with institutions like the Stanford Research Institute, spanned from the 1970s until its declassification in 1995.

While the Stargate Project was eventually terminated because of questions about its efficacy, its existence underscores a period when government agencies earnestly explored the boundaries of human perception and consciousness.

NASA's Remote Sensing: Science and Perception

In contrast to the metaphysical approach of remote viewing, NASA employs "remote sensing" as a scientific method to collect data about Earth's surface and other planetary bodies. This technique involves the use of satellite or airborne sensor technologies to detect and classify objects on Earth or in space by means of propagated signals. Applications of remote sensing include monitoring environmental changes, mapping planetary surfaces, and assessing meteorological hazards.

While distinct from psychic practices, the terminology and objectives of NASA's remote sensing initiatives echo a shared human desire to perceive and understand realms beyond our immediate experience.

Intersecting Realms: Science and the Paranormal

The juxtaposition of governmental interest in both psychic phenomena and advanced scientific observation techniques highlights a broader narrative: the enduring human quest to transcend limitations and access deeper layers of reality. Whether through the lens of science or the exploration of consciousness, these endeavors reflect a commitment to expanding our understanding of the universe and our place within it.

For further reading on the Stargate Project and NASA's remote sensing programs, consider exploring the following resources:

- Remote Viewing - Wikipedia

- Stargate Project (U.S. Army unit) - Wikipedia

- Remote Sensing - NASA Earthdata

- Remote Sensing Specialist - MyNASAData

Keep your journal close and your supportive friends nearby. Take notes. Investigate. Research. But above all, open your heart and mind to the unexplained. Trust that your child's gifts—and your love—will guide you both toward healing, understanding, and profound connection.

Being a good parent to a psychic child is not about possessing psychic powers yourself. It is about the courage to love, to listen, and to walk beside your child through the mysteries that only they can see.

"Empaths did not come into this world to be victims; we came to be warriors. Be brave. Stay strong. We need all hands-on deck."

—Anthon St. Maarten

How Do I Find Out If My Family and I Have Psychic Abilities?

Leitreanna's Reflection

I am the fourth generation that I know of, of psychic mediums in my family. The roots run deep, like an ancient tree whose branches reach into the unseen realms. When I hear families ask, *"Where do our psychic origins come from?"* I feel that profound resonance because I, too, have sat with that very question. It is natural to wonder where these gifts come from, and more importantly, how to recognize them in ourselves and those we love.

So, first, take a deep breath. Let it fill your lungs slowly—and then release it with intention. Take another breath, just like that. You are safe here. You will find answers, or perhaps many answers, along this journey. Because I can tell you this with certainty: you and your family *have* spiritual abilities.

That you are drawn to this question means the spirit world is already whispering your name.

From what I have seen, psychic gifts rarely look the same from person to person—even within the same family. Each gift is as unique as the individual's fingerprint; a divine signature etched into their soul. Some may see visions; others might hear whispers or feel presences. Some might have healing hands, while others walk between worlds in dreams. And that is okay. This diversity of experience is part of the sacred tapestry that makes up our family.

Did you know, according to www.todaygov.com, that one in every three people claims to have experienced some form of psychic phenomenon? And nearly thirty-eight percent of U.S. adults say they have felt a ghostly presence at least once. Belief or disbelief does not shield anyone from the spiritual realm's touch—it moves beyond human logic and reason.

When I was about four years old, my grandmother sat me down and shared a secret only the women in our family knew. She said, *"Our ladies see things. They know things."* I did not understand what that meant at first. How could someone just *know* things? It seemed impossible for a little girl like me.

Later, she told me stories that made the air feel thick with mystery. She spoke of my great-grandmother, who once came to help a frightened child. This child saw a man—an older gentleman in a cardigan sweater—standing silently in the corner of the room. No one else could see him. The child refused to be alone in the house, terrified. But my great-grandmother could see the man too. She knew he was the previous tenant of that home, still lingering in the shadows of the past.

As I listened, a queasy feeling rose in my stomach—not fear, exactly, but a mixture of awe and trepidation. How could I be brave enough to face something so otherworldly? Yet, it was part of my heritage.

Mama Jenny, my grandmother, also shared stories about Mom—the woman who saw angels. Mom described an angel so beautiful and loving that it filled her young heart with peace. Mom's gift of prayer and healing began when she was just four years old. People from the church would come to our house, calling or visiting, asking her to lay hands on them and pray for healing. This was not a secret or a hobby, it was a sacred calling.

I remember the way Mama Jenny spoke of these encounters with such admiration and reverence. It was clear she held a deep respect for both the women in our family and the spiritual world they navigated. Mama Jenny was my first guide, introducing me gently to a reality that often remains hidden to others—a reality where spirits touch our lives and remind us of the unseen.

But I still wondered: *How would the spirit world touch me?* When I turned six, my mother began teaching me how to pray like an adult, how to speak to the unseen with faith and intention.

Like many children, I quickly learned to pray for my loved ones, but my mother's gift was extraordinary. One day after school, I took a nap before dinner. When I awoke, the smell of one of my favorite meals drifted into my room. Yet, the scent made me queasy, and soon I realized I was extremely sick. The doctor gave me medicine, but instead of feeling better, I grew worse having an allergic reaction to the medicine.

What happened next would have been easy to dismiss as a fever dream or hallucination to anyone else, but I knew better. I also knew my family would not flip about my supernatural experiences; they would honor them, hone them, and look for more details. I knew I was safe with them by my side. When I had my first supernatural experience, I realized what I saw was real. Not once, but several times. I was surrounded by light and presence, protected and comforted. I never felt alone or strange in those moments because my family believed me. They held space for my experiences without question.

We never spoke of these things openly in public— there is too much misunderstanding and ridicule out there. People often laugh or mock what they cannot comprehend. But my grandmother once told me something important: *"Those who mock or dismiss what they do not understand will be the first to seek your help when their world breaks apart."*— *Virginia Scott.*

Our gifts are not just for us—they are a bridge to help others awaken to mysteries beyond their knowing.

Mama Jenny, and Mom said our spiritual gifts are a divine calling to assist those who cannot relate to the paranormal. We become messengers, guides, and healers, introducing others to the possibility that life is much larger and more beautiful than what we can see or touch.

As I share my family's story, I hope it touches your heart and stirs memories of your own. You recall a moment when a relative just "knew" what to say or was in the right place at the right time, like some grand cosmic plan. Perhaps you have noticed a love story between grandparents that felt like a fairytale destined by fate. Your ancestors were soldiers or first responders carrying unseen scars and memories no logic can explain.

I encourage you to listen to those stories. Record them. There are nuggets of psychic wisdom hidden in family lore, waiting to be uncovered. Look for common threads in your family's experiences and your own. The patterns will emerge.

Another way to discover your family's spiritual gifts is to keep a dream journal alongside a journal of thoughts, feelings, and intuitive hits. Write down your predictions, your strange dreams, and moments of knowing. When events unfold, review your notes. Over time, you will see patterns that encourage your curiosity and deepen your connection to the unseen.

Remember, you are not alone on this journey. The spirit world is reaching out to you and your family right now, inviting you to awaken, to listen, and to step into a greater understanding of who you truly are.

Was My Family Different?

Was my family different from others? Perhaps. While many grew up with bedtime stories rooted in fairy tales or cartoons, I was raised with truths that whispered of another world—a world where the supernatural was not only real, but ever-present. In our home, the veil between realms was acknowledged, respected, and sometimes lifted.

From a youthful age, I was drawn to the mysteries that lie beyond the physical. My curiosity was not just encouraged, it was cultivated. Ghosts, spirits, cryptids, and unseen energies were not myths in our house; they were part of life. I had my first ghostly encounter before my first cryptid sighting, and both occurred so closely together that I now know it was no coincidence. My family told me I was being *seasoned*—prepared by Spirit for a life of deeper seeing, deeper knowing.

We believed—and still believe—that God bestows these gifts with purpose. They are not for spectacle or fear, but for service. We are meant to use them to help others, to protect, heal, and guide. Spirit communicates constantly. And the messenger? It could be a dream, an animal, a shadow in the corner of your eye, or even a stranger's casual word. But always, always: God is in control. Over animals. Over spirits. Over all beings, whether in this world—or beyond it.

Testing Spirits: Discernment is Protection

Even in spiritual service, not all that glitters is divine. I was taught to *test the spirits*—a practice rooted in ancient scripture and spiritual discipline.

1 John 4:1 tells us:

"Beloved, do not believe every spirit, but test the spirits to see whether they are from God, because many false prophets have gone out into the world." (Bible).

To test a spirit:

- **Ask the spirit to identify itself**. A true spirit of light will never lie or evade.

- **Ask if they confess Jesus Christ came in the flesh** (1 John 4:2). Deceiving spirits cannot affirm this truth.

- **Check the emotional and energetic signature** of the spirit. Divine presences bring peace, clarity, and love—not confusion or fear.

- **Pray or use sacred words** in your tradition—like reading from Psalms or reciting protective mantras. Negative spirits will flee from divine authority.

Trust your instincts, but verify through prayer and grounding. Discernment is the psychic's shield.

The Science of Inheritance: Epigenetics and Spiritual Sensitivity

You might wonder—are these gifts purely spiritual, or is there also something biological? The answer may be both. Enter: **epigenetics**.

Epigenetics is the study of how behaviors and environment can cause changes that affect the way your genes work—**without altering the DNA sequence itself**. ("Epigenetics Counseling & Consulting: Libertyville Mental Health …") These changes can be passed down through generations, meaning the *experiences of your ancestors* can influence your current reality.

For example:

- Trauma can leave epigenetic markers, increasing stress reactivity in descendants.

- Conversely, strong spiritual practices or deep intuitive experiences can shape

neurological sensitivity in future
generations.

This science helps explain why psychic gifts often run in families. If your grandmother was a dream walker or your uncle saw spirits, you may have inherited not just a spiritual legacy—but a biological predisposition to perceive what others cannot.

📚 Sources:

- CDC: What is Epigenetics?

- NIH: Epigenomics Fact Sheet

- Yehuda, R. et al. (2016). *Holocaust Exposure Induced Intergenerational Effects on FKBP5 Methylation. Biological Psychiatry.*

A Sacred Responsibility

If you were raised like me, knowing the world is more than what we can see, then you understand the weight of this path. But if you are only now awakening to it, know this: your journey is just as sacred.

Gifts come when we are ready to carry them and each vision, whisper, "impossible" moment, is a thread in the tapestry of your divine calling.

You are not strange. You are not alone.

You are *chosen*—and your ancestors are watching.

"Journal writing, when it becomes a ritual for transformation, is not life-changing but life-expanding." ("10 Insanely Powerful Reasons Why Journaling Benefits Your Life") Jen Williamson

Does My Child Have Spiritual Gifts? How Would I Know? Are There Signs?

Blaine's Reflection

Most children today are born with intuitive and spiritual gifts, sometimes subtle, sometimes striking. These gifts are a different kind of intelligence, unlike reading, writing, or arithmetic. It is a new form of knowing, a deeper way of understanding the world and the unseen threads that weave life together. For many parents, this can be confusing, even overwhelming. But once you learn what to look for, recognizing your child's intuitive and spiritual gifts becomes a gentle, beautiful discovery.

The children we raise today, the ones who seem to sense more, feel more, and dream more, are part of a generation awakening to a new kind of intelligence. It is common, yet still deeply mysterious. It is important to remember: each child's gift is unique, like their fingerprints or the timbre of their laughter. Your child's gifts will not look exactly like anyone else's. But they will be unmistakably theirs.

Here are some signs and questions to gently guide you:

- Is your child unusually sensitive—able to pick up on feelings, moods, or energies around them, even if they do not say so aloud?

- Does your child show extraordinary creativity or analytical thinking, or express themselves in ways that seem beyond their years?

- Is your child a deeply imaginative or "right-brain" thinker, often lost in their own world of vivid ideas and visions?

- Does your child ever get "vibes" from people, places, or situations, sensing something unseen or unspoken?

- Does your child seem overwhelmed by crowds, loud noises, or chaotic environments?

- Has your child ever said they have been somewhere before, even if you know it is their first time there?
- Does your child have an imaginary playmate or say they hear voices no one else can hear?
- Does your child share details about deceased relatives or historical figures who once lived in a place?
- Has your child told you they see ghosts or spirits?
- Does your child experience flashes of light, unexplained noises, or strange occurrences that defy explanation?
- Is your child especially drawn to animals or seems to have a unique way with them?
- Can your child see auras—colored energy fields around people or objects?
- Does your child have incredibly vivid dreams, sometimes seeming like visions or premonitions?

If you answered yes to even a few of these questions, it is likely your child is experiencing an *awakening*—the emergence of psychic or spiritual gifts beginning to surface in their life.

For parents, this realization can bring up many questions and sometimes worry. You want to nurture your child's gifts without fear or confusion. Before we dive into the *how* and *what* of intuitive development, there is a profound truth to hold in your heart:

Intuitive development and spiritual giftedness are two sides of the same coin.

If you walk the path of intuitive development long enough, you will become more spiritually aware. If you commit to spiritual practice, your intuition will sharpen. These abilities arise from the same source—a higher power, divine intelligence, or universal energy, whichever name feels right to you. Travel far enough down one path, and you will find yourself on the other.

Therefore, moving beyond labels like "psychic," "medium," or "intuitive" is essential for your child's growth. Their gifts may shift, morph, or emerge in new ways as they grow. What appears as clairvoyance today might evolve into healing abilities tomorrow. Some children pause their abilities during hormonal shifts and then return stronger than ever. Spiritual maturity, in a way, is like *getting an upgrade*—a deepening and expanding of their inner capacities.

This can be hard for parents, especially when you want certainty and clear milestones. But remember, we are evolving—not just biologically through our DNA, but spiritually through our environment and experiences. Families grow together in these ways, nurturing one another in love and understanding.

To help you understand what your child might experience, here are ten core intuitive abilities to watch for. These are not boxes to check but doorways into the richness of your child's unfolding spirit:

1. Clairsentience: This is the art of intuitive feeling. Clairsentient children pick up on the energy of people, places, and situations deeply. Imagine a child who can walk into a busy room and immediately feel

overwhelmed or drained. They might even hold an object and tell you its story without ever seeing its history. This is psychometry—the ability to "read" energy imprinted on things.

2. Clairaudience: The art of intuitive hearing. Children with this gift hear things beyond normal sound—voices, music, or messages from spirit guides or angels. This can sometimes be mistaken for imaginary playmates or even mental illness if misunderstood. Listen carefully and compassionately. These experiences are often beautiful gifts needing gentle guidance.

3. Clairvoyance: The art of intuitive seeing. Clairvoyant children receive images, visions, or "movies" in their mind's eye. They might describe places, events, or people they have never met, offering glimpses into other realms or past lives.

4. Claircognizance: This is knowing without knowing how you know—an instant download of information or understanding. It is that sudden insight when you just *know* something is true without explanation. Imagine your child solving puzzles or answering questions with a certainty that surprises even you.

5. Clairgustance and Clairtangency: Tasting or touching sensations linked to psychic input. For example, a child might taste a flavor or feel a texture out of nowhere, connected to a spirit message or intuitive clue.

6. Precognition: The ability to sense or dream about events before they happen. Your child might have vivid dreams that later come true or a sudden feeling about what is going to unfold.

7. Empathy: Not just emotional sensitivity, but deeply absorbing others' emotions as if they were their own. Empathic children need

exceptional care to protect their emotional boundaries.

8. Mediumship: Communicating with spirits or ancestors. This might manifest as conversations with deceased relatives or unexpected knowledge from beyond.

9. Healing Abilities: Some children naturally soothe pain or anxiety with their touch or presence, even without understanding the power behind it.

10. Psychometry: As mentioned, the ability to hold or touch objects and receive intuitive information or impressions about their history.

These gifts, like the colors in a prism, are many and varied. Your child may show signs of just one or many, and the intensity will change as they grow. As you begin this journey, take moments to observe family interactions, conversations, and the unexplained moments. Keep a gentle journal of these experiences and discuss them with your child in a loving and open way. You are now a detective of the heart and spirit—watching for clues, patterns, and signs.

Above all, remember this: your child's gifts are a sacred trust. They are a doorway to deeper understanding, compassion, and connection—not just to the unseen world, but to the family and community that will support their growth. Nurture their gifts with love, patience, and curiosity, and watch as they bloom into the remarkable beings they were always meant to be.

"Children are spiritual beings that come through you, not for you."- Dr. Wayne Dyer.

The Ghost Gwen Never Asked For

Gwen Johns never liked the family farmhouse. There was something about the way the walls creaked when no one was moving, how the windows always seemed to sweat in the corners, even when it wasn't humid.

After her parents divorced, her father made a surprising choice—he moved them into that very farmhouse. Her uncle had once joked that the place was haunted by "dead farmers too stubborn to leave."

At first, she thought it was just the loneliness of the house that unsettled her. But one evening, something changed.

She saw him.

A man—silent, still—standing near the barn door. His clothing was torn and smeared; his eyes sunken yet somehow seeing.

Gwen froze. It felt like the air itself stopped moving. Then, as suddenly as he had appeared, he was gone.

Her father didn't believe her. He scolded her for being dramatic, accused her of making things up. The more she tried to explain, the more embarrassed she became. So, she stopped. She buried it.

But years later, at a family reunion, Gwen overheard a conversation that shook her: her great-grandfather had died on the property in a gruesome accident. The way they described it matched exactly what Gwen had seen that night.

She hadn't imagined it.

She had witnessed something real. Something no child should have to experience alone.

The Woman in the Cemetery

Across the state, another child was having a very different—but eerily similar—experience.

Blaine was spending the night at his grandmother's house. Her home sat just across the street from an old cemetery, quiet and still beneath the moonlight.

One night, drawn to the window by a strange feeling, Blaine spotted a woman sitting on a gravestone. She was crying with her head in her hands, shoulders shaking.

Feeling an overwhelming need to help, Blaine went outside, crossed the road, and softly asked her if she was okay.

The woman looked up and smiled.

She told him she would be, because someone like him had cared enough to ask.

Blaine smiled back, feeling like he'd done something important, something kind. But then, just as he blinked, the woman faded—vanished into the night air like fog lifting at sunrise.

Shaken and wide-eyed, Blaine ran back to his grandmother's house and told her everything. She listened, her face unreadable. Then, to his surprise, she said she'd seen the same woman before.

"I'm relieved you saw her, too," she whispered. "But don't ever tell anyone else, Blaine. Not ever."

In that moment, something inside him shifted. What began as a beautiful encounter became a source of confusion and shame.

Blaine didn't understand why—but he felt as though he had crossed an invisible line. And now, like Gwen, he would carry this secret in silence.

The Weight of Being Different

Both Gwen and Blaine had been born with gifts—abilities that allowed them to glimpse beyond the veil, to sense what others could not. But instead of nurturing those gifts, the adults in their lives silenced them.

- They were made to feel *strange*.
- They were taught to hide a part of themselves away from the world.
- They were burdened with the belief that what made them special could also make them unacceptable.

It would take years before either of them would find the language to describe what they experienced—time slips, spirit communication, psychic echoes. It would take longer still to accept they weren't broken or cursed.

They were gifted.

Finding the Circle

Eventually, both Gwen and Blaine found others who had seen what they had seen—who had grown up with spiritual sensitivity and *support.*

Judy, Matthew, and Leitreanna had been raised in families where psychic abilities weren't shamed but celebrated.

Their parents and grandparents asked questions, encouraged exploration, and built a foundation of trust around spiritual experiences.

When Gwen and Blaine met them, it was like being welcomed home.

They talked freely about what they saw, what they felt, and what they had been afraid to say for so long.

They learned that there was no shame in sensitivity, and they discovered that being different didn't mean being alone.

And through that bond, they began the lifelong work of healing the wounds of silence—and honoring the power of their inherited gifts.

Reflection Journal: Reclaiming What Was Hidden

Were you ever told to hide your inner knowing?

Maybe it came as a warning — "Don't talk like that," or "People will think you're crazy."

Maybe it was silence—when no one acknowledged what you saw, heard, or felt.

Maybe you simply learned that your truth was unwelcome.

Do you know how to reclaim the truth of what you saw?

Reclaiming it starts with permission—from yourself.

Permission to believe what you felt.

To revisit the memory without judgment.

To write it down, say it out loud, or share it with someone who understands.

In this space, you are not alone.

🔲🔲 *Write below about a time you saw or felt something real—but were told to ignore it. What would you say now to your younger self in that moment?*

"How do I protect my child from people that will not understand or from negative entities?"

Judy Terry—Leitreanna Brown answers,

When you deal with psychic children, their spiritual well–being must also be protected. Reports seem to come from every direction describing how children have been victimized and exploited from sources that parents usually trust, such as coaches, pastors, daycare workers, and health care professionals.

As we process protective measures for our children in their day-to-day life, parents and grandparents of psychic children have a much larger task of protecting their psychic children.

Not only does the child need protection from spirits and psychic knowledge, but they need protection from society's judgmental eyes. What if someone lost their parent or sibling? Talking to their deceased loved one would be everything to them! If your child has the pressure of passing adult communications from spirit to strangers, the scenario can be scary!

Having a psychic child that sees and hears spirits talking to them about their adult life in the past exposes your young child to adult memories, questionable information, potentially unscrupulous ghosts, and harsh environments that cause psychic kids to grow up fast.

There is no problem with that because our creator allowed your child these abilities. But the question remains, how can parents protect their children during spiritual encounters?

Adults often subscribe to religious doctrine, and these creeds affect how parents react to supernatural episodes. Religious dogma can be positive for the entire family and helpful when dealing with psychic talents. Protective prayers help the whole family proceed with caution. On the other hand, religious doctrine is often deemed absolute, and if the parents feel the psychic child is having episodes that are not aligned with family beliefs, the child is scorned and suppressed.

The best-case scenario is to use caution, cling to the protection the family believes in, and then be open-minded, even analytically, about supernatural encounters.

Let us break this whole scenario down into smaller bites.

You need to value the gifts your child has. Children need encouragement and love. Rewarding moments are treasures for family—the awakening of a psychic changes everyone around them. So many times, I have seen an entire group of people awakening as an event. When chaos swirls in the world around us, the supernatural abilities of people peak and strengthen.

Just as indigenous people from history used psychic powers to protect themselves, watching the enemy from a distance and sizing up their threat, we can utilize our abilities to determine horrific natural disasters, illnesses within the family unit, and exciting premonitions that tell something great is about to happen, just for starters. The family remains prepared, protected, and gifted.

Unfortunately, not all children have caregivers involved in their lives to lead or protect them, so they do not realize what is happening to them.

These lost children often lean hard into their supernatural experiences because they are left alone to deal with their own lives.

My older, deceased family members believed childhood hardships increased their magical abilities. Let's face it, when children need someone, and they have nobody, it is an open door to allow unsupervised spiritual experiences to occur, and these types of cases can often take over a child's life.

Many times, people ask me why ghosts and scary spirits target young children. Consider this: neglectful situations hurt children because they are developing their psyches. They are deciding if they can trust the people around them. They build their self-worth, or self-esteem, by how their parents and other caregivers treat them. Much later in life, a person adjusts to the realities of their self-esteem by comparing their childhood and adulthood.

Honestly, some people never heal from the wounds of their childhood. It is safe to assume that neglected or abused children live in a hostile environment. Is their overall mindset also negative?

With that in mind, let us also face that a psychic is on the supernatural interdimensional spectrum, and negative energy attracts "like-for-like" energy.

Now you understand the dangers of mystically talented children awakening their talents alone. The abuse and neglect can include abuse from supernatural forces.

In these cases, where a child needs supernatural intervention, Blaine, Gwen, Matthew and I step in to turn the lives of all involved around.

Did you know that people with negative spiritual experiences as a child often pass that experience on to their children?

The same spirits that harassed adults when they were children will also see their offspring as prey. We call the cycle of spiritual negativity a generational curse.

Wouldn't it be better if your child could approach parental figures with information without fear? Wouldn't it be better for parents to experience these adventures as a family?

By "showing up" for your child, with whatever love and abilities you have, to help them sort out their gifts, feelings, and challenges, you nurture them, and they feel validated.

My grandma said that "lost children psychics" are often given their abilities by God so that they can have what they need to adapt to their hardships in life. My grandma was an abused and neglected child with negative spiritual experiences. She stood up to the negative entities that appeared and ran them out of her home at twelve years old.

She was completely alone as a young child through her teenage years, yet something within her knew she could stand on authority and conquer the menacing spirits that tried to take her over.

For Mama Jenny, her life purpose came early. She found ways to stand up to spirits and stood up to people who were unfair to her. She would do anything for the people she loved. She said when someone discovers their true strengths; they empower themselves to take authority for their best life.

As the child racks up more of these spontaneous psychic experiences quickly over a brief period, it can induce habits such as publicly talking to themselves when talking to spirit. That habit of curiously talking in thin air can cause social rejection. After all, that would look mighty strange!

Kids need reminders of how they look to people, and parents can help manage curious behavior that everyday people may perceive as weird. I know parents want to do more for a psychic child, but believing in their sensory powers, protecting them by keeping family secrets, and helping them fit in with society is a significant role!

Another type of protection a child needs is religious knowledge. If an opposing entity surfaces, you exercise your spiritual authority by taking spiritual control of your home.

Do not panic!

Look into the religion you prescribe to. Also, be sure to do some analysis. Change the energy in your home by removing all negative objects, watching comedy movies, or uplifting ones, burning white candles, eating lean and green, and washing with salt water. Do some deduction also, but remember when the first-time negative spirit appeared. Think about the previous three days to look for clues.

- Did someone new come into the home?
- Was there a unique experience that happened?
- Did someone purchase something that came from a hostile environment?

- Did someone from the home experience a malevolent person, a malicious place, or a wicked thing?
- Has anyone made any threats or became erratic recently?

Remember, the people around your family do not have the spiritually developed talents that yours do.

Spirits attracted to the people around you can easily find you and your family. Your family is on the supernatural spectrum; the spirit can be drawn to you or your family members like a moth to a flame. Negative entities can take away any doubt that the spirit world exists. There are lower-level evil spirits to powerful, wicked entities.

In comparison, positive energies of light and love will come to your aid and stand in intercession for your benefit. Become your best self by finding your strengths and knowledge. Your family will thank you, and you might start a new family tradition of spiritual power.

The Soul, The Gift, and The Legacy

"No one can give a definition of the soul, but we know what it feels like. The soul is a sense of something higher than ourselves, something that stirs in our thoughts, hopes, and aspirations, which go out to the world of goodness, truth, and beauty. The soul has a burning desire to breathe in this world of light and never lose it—to remain children of light." ("35 Most Inspiring Albert Schweitzer Quotes - AnQuotes.com,") — Albert Schweitzer, German-Alsatian philosopher, and theologian.

This quote captures the essence of what many families with psychic children experience. These children, guided by their soul's light, often walk between worlds—seen and unseen.

They perceive more, feel deeper, and know things without being told. For their parents, the question inevitably arises: "How do I nurture my child's gifts?"

"How Do I Nurture My Child's Psychic Gifts?"

Judy Terry Responds

I have been blessed beyond measure. I was raised by two extraordinary women, my mother and grandmother, who both possessed profound spiritual abilities.

They did not just teach me how to pray; they taught me how to *listen*, how to question respectfully, how to take spiritual authority when needed, and how to love unconditionally. They passed on tools, not just tales. Wisdom, not just warnings.

That legacy did not end with me. It deepened when I became a mother and continued to blossom when my daughter, Leitreanna, became a mother herself.

When Leitreanna and her husband asked me and my mother to live with them, we all agreed it was more than just convenient, it was *divinely orchestrated*. For over twenty years, we lived under one roof: four generations, each carrying unique threads of spiritual insight and sensitivity. And when my grandchildren's gifts surfaced, we were ready.

From an early age, we saw signs that Leitreanna's children and other family members were tapping into the same spiritual stream. Just as we had done with Lei, we observed their experiences closely. We responded with intention, not fear. We helped them channel their psychic impressions through creativity. They would draw the spirits they saw or illustrate the messages they received from beyond. In our home, spiritual experiences were not suppressed, they were studied.

We taught our grandchildren that being psychic is not just emotional; it is analytical. Each experience had to be examined carefully.

My mother would say, *"Never accept a spirit at face value. Investigate its intent."* We held debriefings like detectives after every occurrence, seeking patterns, symbols, and potential deception.

When Leitreanna was six, we took her to a grocery store owned by Mr. Herbert, a kind man who had experienced paranormal events. We let Lei lead the questioning.

After their conversation, she told us she saw an older woman near him, smiling and winking. It turned out to be his deceased mother, who did not want him to know she was still present. That day, we validated Lei's abilities and helped her trust her inner senses. Years later, Mia and Elijah visited the same store and connected with the same spirit. Across generations, we compared notes and found uncanny consistency.

Psychic parenting is about trust, repetition, and presence. When other kids came over, our grandchildren, nieces and nephews played like all kids—bikes, cartoons, snacks. But when it was just us, that is when the genuine conversations happened.

"There is a psychic cost children bear when they grow up in fear." ("John Niven - There is a psychic cost children bear when… - BrainyQuote,")—John Niven.

Fear is the enemy of intuition. If you suppress a child's psychic experiences, you are teaching them to doubt the very gift that could help them understand themselves and the world.

Children need safe containers to explore their spiritual awareness.

"Where Do I Go From Here?"

Everyone Reacts

If you suspect or know your child is psychic, here are ways to nurture their development:

- Play intuitive games

  Use card games like Go Fish or Old Maid. Hold up a card and ask them to guess what it is. These gentle exercises build confidence in their inner knowing.

- Teach them conscious breathing

  Breathing helps calm the body and sharpen awareness. It teaches kids to differentiate between their own emotions and impressions they may be picking up from others or the spirit world.

- Help them tune in (and out)

  Teach them to recognize the difference between imagination, thought, and genuine psychic communication. This discernment is foundational.

- Start with aura readings

  Have your child draw your aura using crayons. Then ask them to explain each color and feeling. What do they sense? What emotions come through?

- Let them draw what they see

  If they describe seeing spirits or receiving messages, encourage them to draw these impressions. Over time, you may see recurring symbols or figures.

My Family Was Different

Leitreanna & Judy

Was my family different from others? Perhaps. While many grew up with bedtime stories rooted in fairy tales or cartoons, I was raised with truths that whispered of another world—a world where the supernatural was not only real, but ever-present.

In our home, the veil between realms was acknowledged, respected, and sometimes lifted.

From an early age, I was drawn to the mysteries that lie beyond the physical. My curiosity was not just encouraged, it was cultivated.

Ghosts, spirits, cryptids, and unseen energies were not myths in our house; they were part of life. I had my first ghostly encounter before my first cryptid sighting, and both occurred so closely together that I now know it was no coincidence.

My family told me I was being seasoned—prepared by Spirit for a life of deeper seeing, deeper knowing.

We believed and still believe that God bestows these gifts with purpose. They are not for spectacle or fear, but for service. We are meant to use them to help others, to protect, heal, and guide. Spirit communicates constantly.

It could be a dream, an animal, a shadow in the corner of your eye, or even a stranger's casual word. But always, always, God is in control. Over animals. Over spirits. Over all beings, whether in this world or beyond it.

Testing Spirits

Discernment is Protection

Even in spiritual service, not all that glitters is divine. I was taught to evaluate the spirits—a practice rooted in ancient scripture and spiritual discipline.

1 John 4:1 tells us:

"Beloved, do not believe every spirit, but test the spirits to see whether they are from God, because many false prophets have gone out into the world." (Bible).

To test a spirit:

- **Ask the spirit to identify itself**. A true spirit of light will never lie or evade.

- **Ask if they confess Jesus Christ came in the flesh** (1 John 4:2). Deceiving spirits cannot affirm this truth.

- **Check the emotional and energetic signature** of the spirit. Divine presences bring peace, clarity, and love—not confusion or fear.

- **Pray or use sacred words** in your tradition, like reading from Psalms or reciting protective mantras. Negative spirits will flee from divine authority.

Trust your instincts, but verify through prayer and grounding. **Discernment is the psychic's shield.**

More About the Science of Inheritance

Epigenetics and Spiritual Sensitivity

As we discussed near the beginning of the book, psychic and intuitive abilities often appear to run in families. But you might still wonder, are these gifts purely spiritual in nature, or could they also have a biological basis?

The answer, increasingly supported by science, appears to be **both**. This fascinating intersection is being explored through the field of **epigenetics**.

Epigenetics is the study of how your behaviors, life experiences, and environment can modify the way your genes are expressed, without changing the DNA sequence itself. These epigenetic modifications can act like biological switches, turning genes "on" or "off," and remarkably, these changes can be inherited.

In other words, the emotional or spiritual experiences of your ancestors may have left biological footprints that now shape your own sensitivities, perceptions, and inner knowing.

How This Relates to Psychic Sensitivity

Emerging research reveals that intense emotional or spiritual experiences, especially trauma, can alter genetic expression in ways that persist across generations. This includes:

- **Trauma and Fear Conditioning**: Descendants of individuals who experienced severe trauma (such as Holocaust survivors) have been shown to carry **epigenetic markers** linked to increased stress reactivity and emotional processing (Yehuda et al., 2016).

- **Spiritual Conditioning and Intuitive Perception**: While still being explored, there's growing speculation that just as trauma can prime the nervous system, positive, transformative spiritual practices, like deep meditation, energy healing, or regular intuitive work, may also enhance neural plasticity and heighten sensitivity to spiritual and energetic phenomena in descendants.

So, if your grandmother was a dream walker, your great-aunt channeled spirits, or your father had uncanny intuition, it's possible that you inherited more than just family stories, you may be carrying biological predispositions that help you tune into what others cannot.

This adds a powerful dimension to understanding psychic inheritance: it's not only a spiritual lineage, but also one with potential epigenetic roots.

Sources and Further Reading

- Centers for Disease Control and Prevention (CDC). *What is Epigenetics?*

- National Institutes of Health (NIH). *Epigenomics Fact Sheet*

- Yehuda, R., Daskalakis, N.P., et al. (2016). *Holocaust Exposure Induced Intergenerational Effects on FKBP5*

Methylation. *Biological Psychiatry*, 80(5), 372–380.

- North Carolina State University. *Introduction to Epigenetics*

- Harvard Medical School. *Epigenetics: Fundamentals and Impact*

Inheriting More Than DNA

How Epigenetics May Encode Psychic Sensitivity

Epigenetics challenges the old notion that our DNA is destiny. While your genetic code lays the foundation, epigenetic markers, chemical modifications such as DNA methylation or histone modification—influence how, when, and to what extent certain genes are expressed. Life experiences, diet, trauma, toxins, stress, meditation, and even belief systems can trigger these markers.

Key Scientific Findings Supporting Epigenetic Inheritance

1. **Transgenerational Trauma**:

   - Studies on the descendants of Holocaust survivors showed changes in stress hormone regulation genes, particularly the FKBP5 gene, linked to the hypothalamic-pituitary-adrenal (HPA) axis, which manages stress response (Yehuda et al., 2016).

   - Similar patterns were found in children of women exposed to intimate partner violence during pregnancy. Their offspring showed epigenetic changes in the NR3C1 gene, another key stress regulator.

2. **Animal Studies Demonstrate Memory Transmission**:

o   In a 2013 study by Dias & Ressler, mice were conditioned to fear the smell of cherry blossoms. Their offspring, and even the third generation, showed aversive reactions to the scent, despite never being exposed to the original conditioning. This indicated that the trauma memory was passed epigenetically via changes in sperm RNA and DNA methylation.

3. **Meditation and Positive Epigenetic Shifts**:

   o   Recent studies have shown that mindfulness meditation can result in measurable epigenetic changes. For example, experienced meditators demonstrated reduced expression of pro-inflammatory genes and increased activity in genes associated with neural plasticity and repair (Kaliman et al., 2014, *Psychoneuroendocrinology*).

- o This raises an exciting possibility: Could repeated intuitive practices like energy healing, astral projection, or spiritual channeling prime gene expression in a way that's passed down?

Epigenetics and Psychic Families

When looking at families known for their psychic abilities, it's not just folklore that connects them, it may be neurobiology shaped by generations of altered gene expression. These families often share:

- **Heightened sensory perception**

- **Greater limbic system activation**, especially in the amygdala and hippocampus (areas tied to emotion and memory)

- **Increased right-brain dominance**, linked to intuition, holistic thinking, and imagination

If a great-grandmother spent years practicing trance mediumship, her intense neural activation, combined with emotional and spiritual attunement, could theoretically leave epigenetic traces, subtly shaping the nervous systems of her descendants.

You might find yourself naturally attuned to energies, receiving messages in dreams, or picking up on others' emotions without explanation.

That sensitivity may be both learned and encoded.

Nature, Nurture, and the Soul

This scientific lens doesn't diminish the spiritual, it enhances it. Just as a violin can be beautifully handcrafted (genetics) and carefully tuned over time (epigenetics), your psychic sensitivity may result from ancestral experience, environmental input, and soul-level purpose working together.

Your gifts may not only be a spiritual calling but also a biological inheritance shaped by the energy, practices, and emotions of those who came before you.

Additional Sources and Studies

- Dias, B. G., & Ressler, K. J. (2014). Parental olfactory experience influences behavior and neural structure in subsequent generations. *Nature Neuroscience*, 17, 89–96.

- Kaliman, P., et al. (2014). Rapid changes in histone deacetylases and inflammatory gene expression after a meditation retreat. *Psychoneuroendocrinology*, 40, 96–107.

- Zannas, A. S., et al. (2015). Epigenetic regulation of FKBP5 by aging and stress contributes to NF-κB–driven inflammation and cardiovascular risk. *PNAS*, 112(43), E6261–E6270.

A Sacred Responsibility

If you were raised like me, knowing the world is more than what we can see, then you understand the weight of this path. But if you are only now awakening to it, know this. Your journey is just as sacred. Gifts come when we are ready to carry them. And each vision, each whisper, each "impossible" moment is a thread in the tapestry of your divine calling.

You are not strange. You are not alone.

You are chosen, and your ancestors are watching.

The Parent as Guardian of the Gift: Your Sacred Role in Raising a Psychic Child

When your child begins to show signs of psychic sensitivity, dreams that reveal the future, seeing spirits, empathic overload, or an uncanny connection to animals, you have crossed a threshold. This is no ordinary parenting journey.

You are now the guardian of a gifted soul. Entrusted with both nurturing their abilities and shielding their spirit.

You may feel unequipped at first. That is okay. You do not need to have all the answers; you need only the courage to walk beside your child, to believe them, and to grow with them.

1. Believe First, Understand Second

The moment your child shares a psychic experience; your reaction sets the tone for their relationship with their gift.

Skepticism, dismissal, or fear can drive their abilities underground. Validation, on the other hand, builds trust and empowers them to explore safely.

"I believe you." These three words can change everything.

Even if you do not understand what they are experiencing, your belief affirms their reality and creates emotional safety, a crucial foundation.

2. Your Responsibility: Become a Student of the Spiritual

Raising a psychic child means becoming a spiritual researcher yourself. You do not need to be a medium or mystic, but you must be willing to learn.

Your child's journey will be smoother if you are informed, discerning, and spiritually present.

Stay Educated:

- **Read widely.** Study psychic development, energy work, spiritual protection, and religious or cultural frameworks around extrasensory abilities.

- **Know the signs of psychic overload.**
  Sensitivity can mimic anxiety, ADHD, or
  even depression when misunderstood.

- **Understand spiritual discernment.** Know
  how to evaluate spirits (see 1 John 4:1) and
  how to recognize divine vs. deceptive
  energy.

Participate Actively:

- Meditate or pray with your child. Create
  regular grounding rituals that foster
  emotional stability and psychic clarity.

- Explore their abilities together, keep a
  shared dream journal, practice telepathy
  games, or visit spiritually significant
  locations.

- Model spiritual hygiene: energy cleansing,
  shielding, and rituals of intention are as vital
  as brushing teeth in a psychic household.

**3. Protect Their Innocence Without Ignoring
Their Wisdom**

Psychic children often carry old-soul awareness and uncanny insights. They might speak truths beyond their years or feel weighed down by premonitions.

But even so, they are still children. They need your protection; not just from outside forces, but also from the crushing weight of their own anxieties and fears.

Help them set boundaries:

- Teach them it is okay to say *no* to spirits.

- Help them filter which messages to share—and with whom.

- Create sacred space at home where they can disconnect, rest, and just *be* a kid.

4. Get Comfortable with Mystery

This journey is not about control, it is about co-creation with the divine. You are not here to explain everything. You are here to walk hand-in-hand with a child whose inner world may one day awaken your own.

Let your child teach you, too.

Be willing to sit in wonder, to admit what you do not know, and to explore the mystery side-by-side. Because the truth is, when a psychic child is born, the whole family begins to awaken.

Further Guidance:

As a parent of a gifted child, ask yourself regularly:

- Am I giving my child space to share without fear?

- Am I educating myself spiritually and psychologically?

- Am I managing my own energy, so I do not project fear or confusion onto my child?

- Do I have support? (Consider parent groups, spiritual mentors, or trusted counselors familiar with intuitive children.)

You are Not Alone in This

This is more than parenting. It is spiritual stewardship.

By guiding your psychic child with love, structure, curiosity, and faith, you are participating in something ancient, beautiful, and rare. You are not only raising a child, but you are also nurturing a light bearer.

Let that truth ground you, even when the path feels strange.

Let it inspire you to keep learning.

Let it awaken your own forgotten gifts.

Closing Thoughts

The Journey Has Only Just Begun

As we come to the close of *So, You Think Your Kid Is Psychic*, know this: if you picked up this book searching for answers, you were guided here for a reason.

Your child dreams vividly of things yet to happen. Perhaps they speak to unseen visitors. Or they feel everything, the emotions of others, the energy in a room, the whispers in silence.

You are not imagining this.
You are not alone.
And neither is your child.

What you hold in your hands is more than a book. It is a beacon, a companion, a doorway into the mystical world your family is now a part of. You have learned how to recognize psychic traits in children, how to nurture their gifts with love and discipline, and how to protect their spirits while honoring their soul's mission.

You have also begun awakening something ancient within yourself, your own intuitive knowing, long buried but never lost.

But this is just the beginning.

The path of the psychic child is not linear. It spirals through lifetimes, touches hidden dimensions, and unfolds over years of deep inner discovery.

New abilities will emerge. New questions will arise. And as they do, you will need even deeper tools, stronger boundaries, and more expansive knowledge.

So, here is where we leave you… for now.

But do not close the door just yet.

In the next book in this series, we will dive even deeper into the advanced development of psychic children, including past-life recall, mediumship training, telepathy experiments, psychic healing, and spirit guide communication.

We will also explore the secret language of family lineages, soul contracts, and the role of ancient ancestors in shaping your child's spiritual destiny.

If this first book has helped you recognize the spark within your child...
The next one will help you understand the fire they were born to carry.

✦ Stay curious.

✦ Stay grounded.

✦ Stay open to the mystery.

Because the veil is thinner than you think, and your child was born to walk between the worlds.

Get ready for the next book in this Psychic Children's series with Family Spirit.

Raising the Light: Guiding Your Psychic Child Through Advanced Abilities and Spiritual Awakening

What if your child's dreams are more than imagination?

What if their imaginary friend is a spirit guide?

Their fear of water comes from a past life…

Or their healing touch is the echo of an ancient soul?

In *Raising the Light*, we take the next step on the sacred path of parenting an intuitive or psychic child.

This is not just about identifying abilities, it is about developing them with discernment, compassion, and wisdom.

This book is for parents, caregivers, and guardians who know their child is meant for something greater, but do not always know how to help them carry the weight of such a gift.

Inside, you will discover real-world strategies, spiritual practices, and tools from psychic mentors, healers, and intuitive families across generations. You will also learn to awaken your own ancestral gifts and step fully into your role as a guide, protector, and spiritual witness.

Your child is here to light the way. Now it is your turn to walk beside them.

Table of Contents

Foreword

A Letter to the Lightworkers Raising the Next Generation

Chapter 1: Past Lives, Present Gifts

Helping your child understand karmic memories, phobias, and inherited soul missions.

Chapter 2: Spirit Guides and Sacred Companions

How to help your child identify, communicate with, and collaborate safely with spirit allies

Chapter 3: The Psychic Language of Dreams

Symbolism, precognitive messages, and keeping a family dream journal.

Chapter 4: When the Veil Is Thin

Understanding mediumship in children and how to protect them in spirit-sensitive environments

Chapter 5: Telepathy, Remote Viewing, and Astral Travel

Practical exercises for psychic development and out-of-body experiences

Chapter 6: Energy Work and Healing Hands

Teaching young empaths grounding, protection, chakra work, and hands-on healing

Chapter 7: Soul Contracts and the Family Lineage of Light

Exploring the ancestral origins of psychic gifts and how to activate your family's spiritual legacy

Chapter 8: Discernment and Danger: When the Spirit World Is Not Safe

How to teach your child spiritual discernment, banishment prayers, and protection rituals

Chapter 9: Building a Sacred Home Environment

Altar building, energetic cleansing, family rituals, and spiritual hygiene

Chapter 10: From Childhood to Initiate

Helping your child transition into adolescence while staying spiritually grounded and empowered

Appendix A: Prayers, Rituals, and Exercises

Family-safe scripts for cleansing, protection, dreamwork, and meditation

Appendix B: Recommended Books, Tools, and Trusted Communities

ABOUT THE AUTHORS

Matthew Brown—The Healer with a Warrior's Heart.

Matthew Brown is a generational psychic, empath, and spiritual protector whose gifts awakened in childhood.

The son of renowned spiritual teacher Linda Fisher, husband to Leitreanna Brown (psychic medium) and son-in-law to the late Judy Terry (psychic and healer.)

Matthew was raised in a family deeply rooted in spiritual tradition. From an early age, he demonstrated a rare ability to read energies, sense danger before it occurred, and soothe others with a healing presence.

He learned spiritual warfare living in a violently haunted home where he did spiritual battle at the age of fifteen years old.

In adulthood, Matthew refined his abilities with a unique balance of mysticism and logic.

Known for his deep empathy and uncanny accuracy, he often receives spiritual messages through dreams, impressions, and sudden knowings.

He serves as a spiritual anchor for children with psychic abilities, helping them feel seen, protected, and grounded in their truth.

As a co-leader of Family Spirit International, Matthew collaborates with his wife and loved ones to provide spiritual education, healing, and guidance to families across the globe.

His specialties include energetic protection, spiritual discernment, and healing through ancestral connection.

Leitreanna Brown—The Matriarch of Mysticism.

Leitreanna Brown is an internationally respected psychic medium, metaphysical educator, and spiritual counselor. A lifelong intuitive and deeply gifted seer.

Leitreanna has spent decades guiding individuals, families, and spiritual seekers through the mysteries of the paranormal world.

Mentored by her mother, Judy Terry, and grandmother, Virginia Scott, she was surrounded by generations of intuitive family members.

Leitreanna's path was written in the stars. Over the years, she has become a beacon for those seeking clarity and connection between the physical and spiritual realms.

Co-founder of Family Spirit International, Leitreanna brings a calm authority and warm wisdom to every case.

She emphasizes ancestral healing, spirit communication, and protection for psychic children, blending her deep intuition with practical knowledge and fierce love.

Judy Terry—Matron of Spirit and Ancestral Wisdom (In Loving Memory)

Judy Terry was the spiritual grandmother of Family Spirit International, a gentle but powerful matron whose legacy of love, wisdom, and spirit continues to guide from beyond the veil.

As Leitreanna Brown's mother and Matthew Brown's beloved mother-in-law, Judy played a pivotal role in shaping the family's spiritual mission.

Her journey into the paranormal began with dreams and ancestral visitations that grew stronger over time.

Judy cultivated a unique ability to speak with spirits, interpret signs, and provide emotional healing to those seeking messages from beyond.

She taught the importance of humility, kindness, and faith in divine guidance.

Judy Terry transitioned from this world in August 2024, but her presence remains palpable to those she touched. Her teachings live on in the hearts of her family, especially in the lives of the children she helped raise in truth and light.

Her voice is now part of the chorus of ancestors who continue to support the Family Spirit mission.

Blaine Rohan—The Truth-Seeker and Protector of Sacred Knowledge

Blaine Rohan is a psychic sensitive, spiritual warrior, and field investigator whose courage and curiosity have defined his spiritual path.

From an early age, Blaine experienced powerful encounters with spirits, cryptids, and energies beyond explanation.

Supported by spirit family like Leitreanna and Matthew Brown, Blaine cultivated a grounded but fearless approach to the supernatural. Guided by spirit and grounded in compassion, Gwen's presence unlocks doors between worlds.

As a vital member of Family Spirit International, Blaine is known for his deep empathy, protective instincts, and unshakable commitment to truth.

He bridges the gap between ancient knowledge and modern methods, helping young sensitive people feel safe and supported.

Blaine specializes in spirit communication, psychic discernment, and working with children who carry powerful gifts.

His work reminds us that bravery in the paranormal world does not come from knowing everything. It comes from walking in truth, no matter what shadows may appear.

He is a voice between the worlds, steady, brave, and divinely attuned.

Gwen Johns

Producer • Advanced Empath • Spirit Communicator

All Access Network Television

Shrouded in mystery and driven by truth, Gwen Johns has walked the fine line between dimensions.

As an empath and medium, Gwen possesses a rare ability to sense, feel, and interpret the invisible threads that bind spirit to soul.

Her gift emerged early, an unspoken knowing, a whisper in the dark, a presence at her side when no one else could see. As a child, she saw spirits long before she had the words to describe them.

Before stepping into the world of media, Gwen served with honor as a first responder, where her intuitive gifts often led her to arrive at the right place at exactly the right moment.

She saved lives not only with skill and training, but with a deep-rooted knowing, one that came from a higher source.

Today, Gwen is the powerhouse producer behind the All Access Network Television podcasts, curating content that pushes beyond the veil and dives headfirst into the unknown.

Her productions fuse investigative truth-seeking with metaphysical insight, exploring everything from psychic phenomena to supernatural encounters.

Whether she's behind the microphone or holding space for the grieving to connect with loved one's beyond the grave, she walks in both the physical and etheric realms with quiet power and sacred purpose.

Together, They Are Family Spirit International

Bound by love, lineage, and legacy, the Family Spirit Team honors the sacred task of guiding families through paranormal awakenings and spiritual mysteries.

With each case they take on, they carry forward the light of those who came before, especially the enduring presence of Judy Terry, whose spirit now walks beside them, offering strength from the other side.

Be looking for books from the other members of Family Spirit International, as they have their own narrative that will touch your heart and mind.